Zhongalish:
Think and Feel Globally

Li Zhimin

Chinese American Association of Poetry and Poetics

Philadelphia

Copyright © 2016 Li Zhimin

Contact: washingtonlzm@yahoo.com (washingtonlzm@sina.com)

Printed in the United States of America

Cover design by Li Zhimin

Published by the Chinese American Association of Poetry and Poetics

3808 Walnut Street, University of Pennsylvania, Philadelphia, PA 19104

on the occasion of Li Zhimin's reading at the Kelly Writers House on October 25, 2016

Published in cooperation with the Segue Foundation.

ISBN: 978-1-93182-466-8

For my mother and father

Who do not read poetry

Whose love leads me to poetry

Content

Foreword: A few stories and a little thinking / 1

I. Prologue: Who am I / 7

II. Feel Words: One Way to Approach Language / 11

III. A Go for Mutual Understanding / 17

IV. Meeting Emily Dickinson / 23

V. Color Politics / 29

VI. A Love of Shining Night / 33

VII. Non-Presence / 39

VIII. Light of America / 45

IX. Charles, my friend of lollypops / 51

X. 曾经（Once） / 55

XI. The most beautiful poem / 73

XII. Epilogue: A Tianist / 77

Afterword / 83

Foreword: A few stories and a little thinking

1. When I was taking a walk with my friend at Swarthmore College yesterday evening, we saw a few teenagers were taking a walk too, in the opposite direction. We saw they saw us. When we were meeting up, two guys raised their left hands and said something like /hai fai/. I did not understand and was confused. But the first idea flashing into my mind is a Nazi salute. I asked, "Sorry?" The guy in the front repeated /hai fai/. My friend saved me! She smiled and said, "Yes! /hai fai/!" And she high fived with the first guy. I suddenly understood and high fived with the second guy. We kept on walking. But I started to feel shameful of myself. In a few seconds, I realized I must have embarrassed the first guy. I looked back at them, and saw a guy looking back at us too. I meant to catch up with them and to say sorry to the first guy. But we were already pretty far away, and it might cause even more embarrassment. I had to swallow up my shame!

I am an English professor. But there is so much that I do not know.

2. I was jogging at Swarthmore College one evening. Suddenly I saw a credit card on the ground. I picked it up, and wandered where to find its owner. It might be too trivial a business to call the police. It should be best to give it to a security guard of Swarthmore College. At this moment, I saw a girl and a boy, probably students, coming over. The boy was pushing a cart. Maybe they could find a security guard for me. I said hello to them and explained what happened. The girl looked at the card and shouted, "Oh! It is mine." And she looked at the boy who was obviously embarrassed. I was relieved, and happy. I said, "You are lucky!" They did not say anything, and I went on jogging. But gradually I felt it might be inappropriate for me to make that remark. I just meant to congratulate them to have got the lost card back. However, my remark seemed to be mocking at them, and it seemed that I was implying I brought them luck which made me seem to be a little bit self-important. I did something good, and I should feel happy. But my silly remark made me feel bad for quite a long time.

    I am an English professor. But there is so much for me to learn.

3. I made a few close friends when I was at Cambridge University in 2001. But I lost two of them just because I made some cultural mistakes that I did not realize until many years later.

I felt awkward. But I had to be content with life.

It is certain that I must have lost many opportunities due to the fact that I do not understand so many cultural rules in English.

But I could only do what I know how to do.

I am happy I am still keeping some friends. I am worrying I might get them lost someday just because some silly cultural mistakes I might make.

I am an English professor. But I am always making mistakes in English.

4. Am I speaking British English, or American English?

My son started to correct my pronunciation of Putonghua when he got six years old, and he has been doing so until now, proudly. In order to defend myself, I argue that I am always making myself well understood, and I am expressing myself most accurately. Therefore, I do not mind having an accent. In fact, I start to feel proud of my accent, which, no matter how hard I work, I could never get rid of. It is inborn. Language is for communication, anyway. So long as I could make myself well understood, it is fine. I sometime even go pretty far to boast that the so-call standard of any language is just something that is to be broken by literary talents. Linguistic rules follow talents. Not the opposite.

But I would still listen to my son and correct myself whenever it is possible.

Am I speaking British English, or American English? So long as I could make myself clear, I do not care what kind of English I am speaking. I do not mind having an accent at all. In fact, I should be proud of it. There is no linguistic authority to judge who is more correct when American English and British English use the same words, such as "football", to refer to completely different things. The only reason is that they will it that way. Their wills count. My will counts too.

Perhaps I shall name my English Zhongalish. By this act of naming, I get my own authority.

In fact, Zhongalish is a new territory where many people reside. Just think of the fact that all students in China have to learn English for six years in the primary school, and another six years in the junior and senior middle schools. We shall build up our own home to make us more independent and feel more comfortable.

5. I would surely learn to make myself well-understood. I would surely learn all the rules governing British English and American English. I would surely pay attention to all the accurate ways, the humorous ways and the beautiful ways of speaking and writing. But I shall not stop here. I shall go even further. In Zhongalish, I could go further. At least, I could take a different road in many cases.

In fact, Zhongalish is not that unfamiliar to a British or an American ear.

When people say "long time, no see," they are speaking Zhongalish, or something originated in Zhongalish.

When Ezra Pound wrote some "ungrammatical" English, judged by the rules of British or American English, in his literary works, he was writing Zhongalishly.

One could hardly see China if one does not recognize Zhongalish. One has to get a little out of the boundary of one own language and culture if one wants to truly "see" and "feel" another culture.

I shall not pretend that I am speaking either British English or American English, though I am always happy to learn from both of them. They are my foundations. Yet I have one more foundation, i.e., the Chinese. I shall frankly admit that I am speaking Zhongalish, though I might not be speaking good Zhongalish that shall be no less accurate, no less humorous and no less beautiful than either British or American English. Or it will get no respect.

Even if I could not write or speak good Zhongalish, by informing people I am Zhongalish, it could save me a lot of embarrassment and troubles, leaving much space for me to revise and improve myself.

Zhongalish is different. And it should be independent.

I shall build up a home for myself, which could be shared by so many of my people. We will be happier when we are not homeless anymore.

2016/08/10

I. Prologue

Who am I

I was born Chinese

I have been learning British and American literatures and cultures

all my life

And Chinese civilization had fused with Buddhism, Islam,

Christianity, Judaism

and many other cultures in the past

And China has been learning western cultures in the modern age

Chinese culture is the outcome of integration of many cultures

I am not a pure Chinese

Nobody is

I am Chinese, as well as American and English

I am a Zhongguo（中国）-American-English person

I am Zhong-a-lish

I live above Zhongguo, America and England

I live under them

Are you born American?

However, if you have learnt the Chinese language and culture, or

if you have ever used anything on basis of the Chinese invention

of printing, gunpowder and the magnet

or if you have used chopsticks

or if you have had any contact with Chinese

or have ever heard some stories of them

Your mentality is somehow changed

no matter how slightly

Thus, in a certain sense, you are Chinese

You are an American Chinese, namely, Americanese

No one is an island

Neither is any people or any race

If one wants to become pure

one has to get rid of all the alien elements of oneself

and, like peeling an onion

nothing is left in the end

It is the intent to communicate with each other

the desire to learn and to be learnt

that makes one great

Like it or not

If one wants to live a decent life

not to become a bigot and to lag far behind

One has to keep open

and to be willing to accept new ideas

and to be ready to change

I am proud of being a Zhongalish

I speak Zhongalish

I think Zhongalishly

And I feel Zhongalishly

I live and die

A Zhongalish

2016/07/05

II. Feel Words: One Way to Approach Language

        1

We have a character for Love

It is AI /ai/ 爱

I know my mother *ais* me the most

But she never says the word *ai*

Never

However

I feel *ai* in her eyes

I feel *ai* in her smiles

I feel *ai* in every word she says to me

I feel *ai* in her voice, her tones and her breath

I feel *ai* in the way she walks

I feel *ai* in the way she stands

I feel *ai* whenever I think of her

…

She does not say it

Never

Yet it is in everything

        everywhere

    2

I met Marjorie Perloff

I do not remember where or when

Yet we started to communicate

She is always very kind to me

She is always ready to give me assistance.

And one day, she ended her email with

"with love"!

I instantly started to feel the word

a once empty word I learnt

from my Chinese-English dictionary

I got involved with a Fulbright program in 2008

and went to visit her at her home

She cooked a delicious dinner for me

She invited a couple of her friends from Princeton University

    to keep me company

    and to drive me to her home

    and back to my hotel

    She was in her seventies

    Yet she cooked for me

    giving me wonderful experience of a warm dinner

Marjorie Perloff entered into the English word of LOVE

in my vocabulary.

        3

Once we came across a word "Chink" at college

We did not know it and checked it up

in an English-Chinese dictionary

We got the meaning there

And a couple of diligent guys

in order to practice their oral English

(*practice makes perfect*, said our beloved English teacher)

started to throw the word all around

at each other

just to practice

and make fun

We did not feel feelings

It is just an empty word to us

And a naughty boy told our English teacher:

we have something equal in Chinese for you too

it is Yangguizi /jaŋguizi/ 洋鬼子

Our English teacher laughed and practiced his Chinese

woshi yige Yangguizi

We all burst into laughter

We discussed on how those words

were coined, or from what kind of

ignorant, fearful and dark minds

We understood them more
but we never felt it
their masters have died out
and their days have passed
perhaps.

    4

It is most difficult to learn the dirty words
of English in China
our teachers never taught them to us
we had to figure them out ourselves
by practicing

We came across the English word "Fuck" one day
We went to our silent teacher, the dictionary
It says "Fuck" literally means
"to make love" or to "have intercourse"
which seems to be very positive
pretty charming and attractive to us

One guy said to another guy

"Fuck you"

The other guy replied

"Sorry! Thank you!

But I only make love with my girlfriend."

We all burst into laughter

No boy dared to try this word on a girl

Neither a girl on a boy

In public

2016/05/12

III. A Go for Mutual Understanding

1

a new baby is born

in the stable

one car come

one car go

two car *pengpeng*

people die

whew--

this was harder than I thought!

2

long time, no see

One, two, three

or none?

I think it is best

if I begin with only one

I will be happy to do three

over the next year.

3

hesitate: he sit & ate

legislate: leg is late

campus: camp us

barren equals to

bar + ren (人)

so that people in the bar are all barren

...

...

I do not want to be

involved with this!

4

it is sort of naive

in writing?

I'll need to rewrite

most of these!

I am not convinced

it is the best use of my time!

one pound for

one error or slip.

5

native or non-native

you me you me

monolingual or bilingual

we two who and who

I give you face

you don't want face

you lose your face

6

are you comforting me?

die away

I will give you some color

to see see

un-ding-able

thank you

know is know

noknow is noknow

7

I hope

I didn't upset him /her?

well, well, well …

a sacred well is a well

that connects to the sea.

communication

starts

8

no wind

no waves

waves in the cup

I shall sit here, serving tea to friends

Chairman Mao said

good good study

day day up

brothers

together up

I will be happy to do this.

August 15, 2011

Note: This poem is the "Editorial Memoir" for the first issue of the journal of *EPSIANS*, published in September of 2011.

IV. Meeting Emily Dickinson

                1

I was introduced to Emily Dickinson
    by Dr. Rathmell at Christ College of Cambridge Univ.
The first poet he read with me.

Thus Emily Dickinson becomes the first poet
    in the book I translated and edited
        and published in China.

Thus I start with Emily Dickinson every year
when I teach poetry in English to my students

At first I did not feel anything much special
    while reading Emily Dickinson
But the more I read
The closer we got

On one morning in 2011
when I was reading Emily Dickinson to my students

The door opened -- abruptly--

I saw Emily Dickinson --

    -- Shining --

       -- Just in front of me!

What a long journey

For me to reach you!

    2

She is white

I am yellow

(as they say)

Should I love her?

What is the color of Love?

She is Christian

I am nothing

(as they say)

Am I allowed to love her?

Love can go without Christianity

Could Christianity go without love?

She is in America

I am in Asia

(as all can see)

May I love her?

Every drop of water in the Pacific

      shall be turned into love

           with love!

She is in the nineteenth century

I am in the twenty-first century

(as all can see)

Could I love her?

Time, time, time

Could it stop love?

3

I had been a slave

of the terror of Death, yet

Emily came up and waved it away

with your shining right hand

I felt your power of peace

    The Power of Peace

I breathed it in

Oh

I breathed it in and in

I grew humble

    and humbler

I became content with myself

    with life itself

I cast no eyes at wealth, or fame, or pride

    or anything

    anymore

I became myself!

I became myself,

myself with

you --

                2016/04/30

V. Color Politics

Is white a kind of color

It is. It is just common sense.

But why is the society

putting white and color against each other?

God creates all different colors to make the world

    a colorful, therefore, beautiful place to live in

How boring it is if the world is just of one color!

Each color is precious, either white, yellow, red

    black, brown, blue, or any other

All colors are equally precious

I do not know why people are classified

    according to their color of skin

Skin is only skin deep

I could never tell who is white

    who is black, who is brown

        not even who is yellow

I was told I am yellow

Yet I have never believed it

When I was a kid

My mother often said I was black in summer

    when the sun is shining hot

and my mother often said I was white in winter

    when the sun is dim and snow is heavy

My mother said I was yellow

    only when I was pretty sick

When she said it

I knew it was time to see the doctor

In a Pennsylvania transportation department

I was asked the color of my eyes

Dark, I replied. I was suspicious why this question was asked.

No, Brown. The guy said while looking straight at my eyes

His strong interest in making it correct somehow

    made me feel a little scared. Something flashed

    into my mind, a scene of Nazi troops

examining people's color of eyes I saw in a movie.

Dark, I said.

But he wrote brown.

I do not know why people are so interested in
      classifying people according to their color
I myself am pretty color blind
And I have never seen anyone who is truly white
      or black, or brown, or yellow
I see each individual for their individual unique color

There are no two leaves that are exactly the same
There are no two people who are of exactly the same color
This is why the world is so beautiful.

How stupid it is to judge one
      in light of one's color
      yet not of one's inner beauty
How stupid to make a friend
      according to the skin color
      yet not of their minds and hearts

Color politics is a stupid game

      played by people who are only skin deep

      for their own stupid political interest

It is a boring game

How boring if people play and

      are made to play it again and again

I see color as Nature sees it

All colors are equal children of Nature

Each color of each individual is an indispensable part of

      the great painting that God paints the world.

                                      2016/07/16

VI. A Love of Shining Night

1

The happiest

man & woman

young & old

am I to be

I have in my hand all my ancestors'

beautiful dreams except my own

modest one

6

They were happy for

they could die &

died

they were happy for

they could

pursue

me

They

hammer boundless vigour

and surging sweat

into a whip

driving hot summers and cold winters

like riding wild horses

flying in clicks and clicks and clicks

I cannot pursue

for I am the summit of summits

the happiest of the happiest

as they wished & worked out

day and night

16

Why they produced so many

beautiful & intelligent instruments

for killing the others and

themselves

as a whole as soon as

they had enough to eat

I see

their shadows growing

evil turns into beauty

it lures sharp edges drink blood dry

it transforms lives into rain bows

I see

heavy dark clouds

piling up in a blue sky

violent thundering & lightening

tearing apart all into

broken guns & rusted bombs

as rain

striking downwards

piercing through all roofs

smashing all cells

in a second

a thick layer of worthless iron & bronze

heaping up on the ground

all is drowned

only a few smoky shadows

escaped into the trembling sky

the earth, out of terror,

was suffocated

17

None of them survived

the radiation dosage is one hundred times

stronger than to kill any organism

they must know

death is the most beautiful

why they created

me suffering lonely in the

world by set-

ting a Clone Pro-

gramme left in a deep

cave that produced

(programme keeps on lying to me

that to rule over the whole world

is the most most most beautiful

shit

shiit

shiii-----------------

t)

I, truly, am not

grateful to them

Note: The original poem was composed in April of 2001 for being presented in the Cambridge Conference of Contemporary Poetry, and was published in 2002. [ISBN: 0-9539986-6-5]

VII. Non-Presence

2

Huge lawns are everywhere

growing on a same spot for centuries

The same spring comes

every year

the same winter departs

every year

with the same beauty

and unchangeable freshness

Lawns can be walked on

by college fellows

Lawns can be viewed

when a college is not closed to visitors

All around are signs

With their owners' titles

Huge trees are occupying huge spaces

leaving no chance for any new beings

A blackbird, who perches on the back chimney of Caius College,

is claiming its territory at dusk

It sings beautifully

A moving mouse breaks his neighbour's privacy

while digging a humble hole

Too small a world!

'apologize'

'no'

Dark crows are waiting in the shade of trees
patiently

Murphy proves that one day
a bad mood of a single person
turns the whole earth
dozens of times
into heaven

Some people think war makes money

'All things in the World are begot from Somethingness
And somethingness comes from Nothingness'
Laozi says, 2,500 years ago

Churches still serve bread and water
But fewer comers

People go travelling a lot nowadays
Hiroshima is a good place to take pictures

A pigeon is drinking in Cam

People like pigeons

6

Macdonald's sprung rapidly all over the nation

Yet it is hard to find a good native American speaker to learn from

Students can communicate in English among themselves

But not with a native English speaker

Chinglish

'Professor,

Train your child

At the very beginning!'

'Why'

'To enter into USA Mainstream'

Ah, ah!

'I spent all my life deposit

but my son has an unchangeable accent----'

A man in two boats

No one is his

'English-learning should begin from baby-hood'

Chairman Mao says, 'Piepie Tide.'

8

'I will come back'

I tell my parents

A beautiful cloud is wandering

Lonely in the sky.

A leaf falls to its root.

Zhuangzi wakes up without knowing

Whether he is a butterfly

Dreaming to be a man

Or a man having dreamed to be a butterfly

Note: This poem is produced by the method of deletion of the poem of the same title published by PennSound in 2009. See: http://writing.upenn.edu/pennsound/x/Li.php.

VIII. Light of America

1

I did not understand why
    so many successful officials and businessmen in China
    had sent their children to America
    or had bought a house here for their retirement life
though some of them were and are blaming
    or even cursing America all the time

Are they stupid or crazy?
They are for sure the smartest people
They are so successful
and they are the only people who could afford to do that
maybe they are just dishonest
or too smart to be understood
    by such ignorant people like me.

But I am always learning
    to understand more of the world
    both externally and internally

2

America was once a barbaric place

So many people were mercilessly murdered

    just because their land was coveted

So many people were brutally enslaved (like animals)

    just because of their color or race difference

So many people were unfairly excluded

    just because of their foreign religious or cultural practice

So many people were violently dispatched

    just because of their gender or sex-orientation difference

    ...

    ...

Yet the light of God gradually

    woke up more and more Americans

    and called on them to fight

    for their own conscience

    for their faith in God

        in liberty, equality, fraternity

    as well as for their brothers and sisters

And they prevailed

And the light of America started to shine

And has been shining till today

This is why so many people are coming over

And more are admiring all around the world

Is there any way to prevent them from coming over

Sure, the best way is to put out the light of America

People have many ways to do that

    and racism that has never really died out

    is certainly the closest way

    to break America down

    and put out the light of America

    altogether.

How sad it would be

if it does happen someday.

3

I am just a poet and a teacher

I could hardly make enough money

    to feed myself and my family

    and to rent a small apartment to stay

I am not qualified to move to America

And I am content

It might be more desirable for me

    to help build up my own homeland into

    a place that shines too

Prometheus stole fire from the heaven

And brought it to light the earth

And even if the fire in Heaven might one day be put out

There will always be light in the universe

China was one of the most civilized nations

    in the traditional age

However, it is just a teenager in the modern age

    easy to be fooled, easy to get excited or to feel hurt

    easy to get offended and annoyed,

    and easy to rise up and break down

America as a nation is of only more than two hundred years
      However its people are from all over the world
      They are in no lack of civilized heritages
America is the big brother in the modern time
    so far, it is dishonest not to admit it
And it does only good to learn the good from a good example

I am just a poet and a teacher
who loves his homeland as well as
    the light of America
What I could do is limited, is humble
I will read some poems in a foreign language I like
    to my students and explain
    why I like them

Would they see the light
and be lit up?

        2016/07/15

50

IX. Charles, my friend of lollypops

1

I met Charles

when I was in the kindergarten

We sat next to each other

We always sat next to each other

Sometimes I brought two lollypops to the kindergarten

and shared them with Charles

I enjoyed it much more when we had lollypops together

I smiled at him and he smiled back at me

Sometimes Charles brought two lollypops to the kindergarten

and shared them with me

We enjoyed it much more when we had lollypops together

He smiled at me and I smiled back at him

Charles stayed with me only for one year

and he moved to somewhere with his parents

more than forty years ago

And we have never met again

I never know why he came
    or why he left
I do not know his family background
I do not know his family name
I even could not remember his face

Yet his name has deeply cut into my mind and my heart
And what I remember is that he likes lollypops
And would share them with me
We are best friends.

    2

When I grew up
I went to college
And I went abroad
I have seen many new faces
And I am always sensitive to the name Charles
But when I offered a lollypop
None of the Charleses I met would take it

It is for children, they said

I started to send emails to friends
I started to post ads in all chatting spots on websites
I am looking for a Charles who likes lollypops
    who would share them with me
    and smile at me.

And I did get responses
Oh, I did.

    3
I have got a homeless Charles
we met in the street
and we had lollypops together
and we smiled at each other

I have got a prince Charles
we met on the internet
and we had lollypops together
and we smiled at each other

I have got a professor Charles

I have got a military Charles

I have got a businessman Charles

I have got a farmer Charles

I have got more Charleses

Charleses of the yellow, Charleses of the White

black Charleses, brown Charleses

and we had lollypops together

and we smiled at each other

My friendship makes no difference in color or race

      no difference in wealth or class

      no difference in gender or age

I select friends with lollypops

I would share them with my friends

and when we have lollypops together

I smile at my friend, and my friend smiles back at me

                2016/07/16

X. 曾经

题记：在费城郊区的小镇斯沃斯莫尔（Swarthmore Ave）附近散步时，偶尔发现了两把椅子，忽然似乎想到了上辈子的经历，颇有触动，于是写成了这一组诗。

1、曾经

曾经
你我相对而坐
你坐在东边
我坐在西边

你的面前是整个西方
可你的眼里只有我
我的面前是整个东方
可我的眼里只有你

2、赠花

我说我最喜欢春天
最喜欢春天里的荷花
你安静地听
你浅浅地笑
你给我背诵《爱莲说》
我也笑了

我说我更喜欢夏天

喜欢夏天的莲蓬

荷花凋谢之后就会长出莲蓬

等到莲蓬越长越丰满

膨胀得像要爆炸了

我就会下水去采摘莲蓬

然后吃掉

你摘了一朵鲜红的花儿送给我

你说你好喜欢

我说我也喜欢

我说我可不是淘气啊

我是真饿啊

十个莲蓬也不够我吃

至少可以垫垫肚子呢

你又送给我一朵雪白的花儿

你让我闻闻

我闻了

好香好香

3、莲蓬

我说莲蓬也有香味呢
闻着莲蓬的香味
晚上我都能笑醒

我摘莲蓬很有经验呢
好几次我在岸上看到一个莲蓬
下水去摘，又在荷叶林里
发现了好几个在岸上看不见的莲蓬

有一次我下水后发现了好多好多
我往前游，发现左边一个
摘了前面的回来摘左边的
摘了左边的，发现左边的左边还有呢
……

4、迷失

我游啊游啊，天都黑了
我不知道岸在哪边了

向前游

　向后游

　　向左游

　向右游

怎么就是游不出去呢

你依然静静地听

你依然浅浅地笑

你说你最爱种花了

我说我也喜欢

我想起大人讲的鬼故事

他们说这就是被鬼下了罩子

我的心砰砰直跳

我想我还是束手就擒吧

我抓着几根粗壮的荷梗

在水面躺了下来

感觉湖水那么温柔

怎么没鬼来抓我呢

它们抓住我

往水里面按一按不就大功告成了吗
是谁在暗中保佑着我呢

我休息了好一会儿
然后我决定只朝着一个方向游

然后呢？你问
然后我就游出了荷叶林了
真聪明，你说
我也无不得意地笑了
……

5、出走

你知道我的理想吗
我的理想是让我的孩子们
不再因为挨饿去摘莲蓬
让所有的孩子们都不再挨饿

于是我出发了
带着你送的两朵花儿

遇到愚昧的人

我让他看

　　　　红色的花儿

遇到迷狂的人

我让他闻

　　　　白色花儿

其实，只要那些聪明人不要

那么愚昧，那么疯狂

什么问题也都会烟消云散了

……

6、重逢

世界真小

原来你还在种花呢！

原来我们坐过的那一对椅子还在那儿呢

　　一张望西，一张望东

我曾经多么希望留下来和你一起种花啊

藤蔓早已覆盖了椅子
一切似乎从未变化

忽然我明白了
原来我一直就留在那儿
和你一起
在花海之中
在人海之中

2016 年 3 月 11 日

Once

While taking a walk at Swarthmore Ave. in Swarthmore on an evening in the spring of 2016, I accidentally saw two chairs, facing each other, covered with ivies. Suddenly it seemed some of my last life experience came back to me. Thus I composed this poem as a record.

1. Once

Once

You and I sat, facing each other

You in the east

I in the west

Before you, it was the whole west

yet you only saw me in your eyes

Before me, it was the whole east

yet I only saw you in my eyes

2. Flowers

I said I like spring

I said I like the lotus flowers in spring

You listened to me quietly

You smiled quietly

I recited to you the prose of "Love of Lotus Flowers"

I smiled too

I said I like summer even more

I said I could not like more of the lotus seeds

When the lotus flowers are gone

lotus seedpods can be seen, growing fast

like the breast of a beautiful girl, growing fast

finally it gets mature, ready to explode at any time

I knew it was time, and plunged into water

to pick up the lotus seeds

and ate them

You picked up a flower of red and gave it to me

You said you love it so much

I said I love it too

I was not naughty at all

I was truly hungry

Even a dozen of lotus seedpods are too little food for me

They could, anyway, relieve me of some hunger

You gave me another flower, a snow-white

You asked me to smell it

I did

It is so fragrant

I am drunk

3. Lotus seedpods

I said lotus seedpods are also fragrant

Thinking of the smell of lotus seedpods

I sometimes laughed to wake up at night

I am pretty experienced in picking up lotus seedpods

For many a time, I saw a lotus seedpod on land

after getting into water, I saw more of them

hiding in the densely scattered lotus leaves

Once I saw more and more of them while in the water

I swam forwards, and found one on the left

after picking up the one in the front

I came back for the one on the left

after picking up the one on the left

I saw more on the far left

...

...

4. Getting lost

I swam and swam.

It was getting dark

I did not know where the land was

I swam forwards

        backwards

        to the left

        and to the right

I just could not get out of the cover of lotus leaves

You listened to me quietly

You smiled quietly

You said you like planting flowers the most

I said I like it too

I thought of the stories of ghosts told by adults

I thought I could have been trapped by ghosts

My heart started to beat heavily

I told myself it should be the best to surrender

I took hold of a few strong lotus trunks

lying on water

The lake water is so gentle and warm

Why weren't there any ghosts coming over to catch me

It was so easy for them to succeed

What they needed to do is to press my head into the water

and all would be finished

Was anybody protecting me, unseen

I took a good rest

and decided to swim just at one direction

What happened? You asked

I swam out of the cover of lotus leaves and saw land

How smart, you said

I smiled, with much pride

...

...

5. On the way

Do you know my dream

My dream is simple

I wish my children do not have to swim

to pick up lotus seedpods to relieve their hunger

I wish all children in the world starve no more

I set out for fulfilling my dream

with the two flowers you gave to me

I show the red flower

to the stupid

    helping them to see it

I show the white flower

to the maniac

    helping them to smell it

In the end, I found it is all because of the smart people

so long as they do not turn themselves

      too stupid or too maniac

so long as they do not make too much trouble

Many of the problems will just vanish naturally

...

...

6. Reunion

The world is so small

And you are still planting flowers

And the two chairs are still there, facing each other

one to the west, one the east

Once I desired so much to stay

to plant flowers with you

The two chairs are covered with ivies

It seems nothing has changed

I start to understand

I have never left

I am in fact always with you

        amid flowers

        amid human beings.

        The original poem was written on 2016/03/11

                and was translated on 2016/07/18

XI. The most beautiful poem

----To each of us, there is one poem that is the most beautiful

/a:/
/a:/
/a:/

/b/
/b/
/b/

爸
爸爸
爸爸爸

香老爸
臭老爸
真是一个臭老爸

豆豆

老豆

这是我老豆

爸,你好!

爸,你好!

爸,你好!

Hello father

Hello father

Hello father

亲爱的老爸

爸爸

爸

/b/

/b/

/b/

/a:/

/a:/

/a:/

April 20, 2016

Note: This poem is one that shall be called as TP-poetry, i.e., transparent performance poetry. Most of it is in Chinese. Yet by performing it, a person who does not know the Chinese language could get the feeling and sense. Thus it is transparent in a certain sense.

XII. Epilogue

A Tianist

> *I am a Tianist*
>
> *Reason and Emotion are my two angels*

1

Am I religious?

That really depends upon how you define religion.

I have my faith, my morals and my ethics.

I like religions that unite people

I do not like religions that separate them

Am I religious?

I am sure I am cultural

I have firm faith in modern cultural values

    such as liberty, equality, democracy, and rule of law

My culture harbors all religions

    that do not go against such modern values

I respect all existing religions in the world
    and admire many of them
I went to many modernized religious places
    that kept their doors to the public
    and prayed there

I could not trust it if someone shows me a book
    and says it records the deeds or will of God
    or says it is of all truth and shall never
    be reinterpreted or revised in the modern age

I could not trust it
    because it is against Reason

I believe all books were written by human beings
I believe there is an angel and a devil in any human
I believe human beings see only what their eyes could reach
    and know only what their age lets them know
I believe human beings make mistakes
I believe there is no book that is divine

I believe in God

I believe God would never speak to any human being

I believe human beings could never truly understand God

In fact, I prefer the term of *Tian* to the name of God

We could see Tian [天]

    in every successful religion

      and in God or gods of them

Yet none of them is Tian itself

Tian has the most beauty

Yet Tian never speaks

Tian has all the truth

Yet Tian never reveals it to anybody

Nevertheless

Tian has kindly bestowed us with

Reason and Emotion

2

I believe human beings are all created by Tian

    all human beings are from the same origin

it is obvious to me because they are of the same bio-structure

    though I am not sure how and why Tian create us

I believe all human beings are of one family

it is obvious to me because they could marry each other

    and produce offspring

Thus they have natural right

    to marry among them

And I believe anybody should marry

    according to one's free individual will

I do not know why human beings had been so much

    scattered and separated in the world in ancient times

Yet since they started to get to know each other in the modern age

    and are able to communicate and meet each other

    in person so easily nowadays

they shall be allowed and encouraged to freely love each other

    and make the family of human beings

    an even more unified, more lovely and more perfect one

People, no matter how separated they are,

    could always be made into a family

      by their children via marriage

I do not believe human beings should destroy each other
though I know they have to compete with each other
    abiding by civilized modern laws
    with their beautiful minds and hearts
    with their honest work
        to win their milk and bread
        to win their sweethearts
        to win respect in the society
        and to win a life in honor of Tian

3

I believe every human being should love their family
    either in the tradition or in the modern
    and should take due responsibilities
I believe every human being should be honest
    and do one's work well to serve the society

I believe, in the modern age, modern values
    serve the society and each of us the best

    and shall be respected and closely observed
I would be happy to pray together with people
    who would follow modern cultural values

I believe every human is created with a divine purpose
    though I am not sure what it is
However, I believe we could find our purposes
    if we open our hearts for emotions to feel
    and concentrate on our minds of reason to meditate
    and work diligently in our daily lives to try hard

I will trust my two angels, Reason and Emotion
    and treat them well
    and work with them well
And live a life of a Tianist.

2016/07/15

Afterword

Zhongalish is born when East and West meet up.

Zhongalish is not British English, not American English. Zhongalish is Zhongalish.

Zhongalish is naturally de-skilled and skillful at the same time.

Zhongalish is a territory that connects East and West, where many people make it their home.

This small poems collection attempts to explore into this virgin territory both linguistically and culturally.

My thanks go to Prof. Charles Bernstein, Mr. James Sherry, Prof. Liu Zhaohui, Dr. Ni Xiuhua and Dr. Zheng Jie for their kind editing or proof-reading work.

www.ingramcontent.com/pod-product-compliance
Lightning Source LLC
Chambersburg PA
CBHW071732040426
42446CB00011B/2324